YOUR KNOWLEDGE HAS VALUE

AF155979

- We will publish your bachelor's and master's thesis, essays and papers

- Your own eBook and book - sold worldwide in all relevant shops

- Earn money with each sale

Upload your text at www.GRIN.com and publish for free

Yehia Abd El Azeem

Muscial Verbalization in the Narrative Diction of Anthony Burgess

GRIN Verlag

Bibliografische Information der Deutschen Nationalbibliothek:

Die Deutsche Bibliothek verzeichnet diese Publikation in der Deutschen National-
bibliografie; detaillierte bibliografische Daten sind im Internet über http://dnb.d-
nb.de/ abrufbar.

Imprint:

Copyright © 2013 GRIN Verlag GmbH
Druck und Bindung: Books on Demand GmbH, Norderstedt Germany
ISBN: 978-3-656-74228-9

This book at GRIN:

http://www.grin.com/en/e-book/280274/muscial-verbalization-in-the-narrative-
diction-of-anthony-burgess

GRIN - Your knowledge has value

Der GRIN Verlag publiziert seit 1998 wissenschaftliche Arbeiten von Studenten, Hochschullehrern und anderen Akademikern als eBook und gedrucktes Buch. Die Verlagswebsite www.grin.com ist die ideale Plattform zur Veröffentlichung von Hausarbeiten, Abschlussarbeiten, wissenschaftlichen Aufsätzen, Dissertationen und Fachbüchern.

Visit us on the internet:

http://www.grin.com/

http://www.facebook.com/grincom

http://www.twitter.com/grin_com

Musical Verbalization in the narrative diction of Anthony Burgess

The two simple words "to compose" have always and still attribute their tonal commitment amongst their listeners and readers to arousing incidentally a fundamental scene of professionalism through which one could play upon his own imagination by way of placing a pointed stick with its accusative didacticism in a grip of a shaggy complexity, or so far -with motifs of symmetry- could recall the rise and fall of uniformed arms in quest for their synchronous guidance. The aforesaid representative of leadership could easily be conceived to be the conductor of masses (the maestro)–who is as much devoted to the very existence of his stick as the writer to his quill-while the former sense of obedience can however be more fit to be imposed on the playing masses, who in concert (though with different aspirations) have always chosen their instruments by which they are objectified. This is but a regular and conventional reflection on music in its performativity, whose many guises –whether instrumentalists, composers, singers or music commentators-would reassert other artists' (writers, painters, architects...etc.) self-satisfaction of music as to be standing in its own rights, composed, played and improvised within its own premises only and by its –musically oriented- attributers. Oppositely, an author who is at the same time a musician in general and a composer in specific, should be considered as phenomenal –a rarity- who in the realm of this introspection is always placed through regular standards of exercise of musical thoughts and judged according to compositional analogies and verbal music in the process of questioning his unusual sort of literature.

Anthony Burgess (1917-1993) is such a writer who was not only a prolific novelist and a longtime literary critic for The Guardian, but also an accomplished musician, composing more than 250 musical pieces and choral works including a single symphony written between 1930/1931 and librettos written and orchestrated by him. Burgess was self-taught in music particularly, although his professionalism in writing came as concerns his own life conditions, spurring him forward to earn a more profitable career than music could by any means afford. In the process of accentuating Burgess musical sensibilities' to his literature – putting in mind his overwhelmingly domineering attractiveness -conceivably experimented in some of his compositions which in terms of musical appreciation always attentive to their textual correspondence- a musicalization of language through which words and their verbosity deviate from the very common forms of verbal articulations and referential associations should be analytically examined in the favor of discovering the ways in which complex allusions/analogies and technical heterogeneity resonate to a greatest extent to the well-versed readings, taking in account references to a variety of instruments and performers, word signifiers and word subjects. Compelling his parents to buy him a gramophone, he continues explaining in his autobiography the comparative propensity he bore to French as much he would henceforward bear to music, stating that "The fact, that I knew enough French by now to understand the title was a kind of confirmation that music too could be intelligible. And, of course, a truth that still astonishes when we care to remind ourselves of it, music transcended language." (Waldman, *A Great and Sustaining Mystery*, 1)

Burgess's individualization of his music in his own texts came as an extended preliminary interaction and reaction he had come through in readings from a number of other modernists who have treated music as well in their own works, mainly James Joyce's "Sirens" episode in *Ulysses* (1922) in which he exemplified tonal characterizations of heroes' voices and aroused musical issues in his dramatizations of textual contrasts and conflicts within characters' personalities and interests. Among other Modern authors who applied music in Literature, were E.M. Forster, Aldous Huxley, Thomas Mann from whom Burgess intensified his realm of musical propensities in language and has proven himself as a a signhood of centralization and decentralization of sound, silence and noise –in which many writers showed specific dedication- and the auditory basis of language, according to which few others showed their only infatuation of musical theory. Burgess's reference for example to one of Joyce's musical writings mainly, the fantasy of "Circe"(429-609) which is the extended Night-town episode of *Ulysses* ,comparing it to symphonic development, is a true manifestation of how he felt the role of music and its auditory elements in the literary works of his counterparts;" Circus may be taken as the development section of the symphonic structure which is Ulysses, and here the breakdown of the time, space and probability encourages Joyce to treat plastically material drawn from other chapters." (JoysPrick 17) In the aforesaid example, "plastically material" could be attributed to sonata forms which depend mostly on extending tones and spatiality away from sharp, inflexible subjects that could be tastefully "broken." This very source of diexis offers in many other summaries the imposition of the "fugal"(a polyphonic composition in which many colors are stated successively as a counterpoint) construction of the "Sirens" episode, where barmaids are presented as a "fugal" subject; to which the "answer" is a character and "countersubject" is another character. Although deconstruction of such polyphonic composition had intended to

2

breakdown its time and space, offering two different voice registers "tenor" and "bass" as another two characters, Burgess could find limitations within its theme, and though he gratified the contrapuntal/counterpoint aspirations of "Sirens", he clarified its impossibility saying that Joyce knows it cannot be done with mere "monadic (having a single vocal part) words."

Burgess, hence, was regularly thinking of writing figures of speech in terms of musical techniques and terminologies, notwithstanding his already acclaimed status of being a musician. It is prominent then to exemplify a first range of a "musicalization" of language in its reference to instruments and voices, inclusive within his writings to presumably untangle musical references and intertwined syntax. It is handy to note that most of references to specific instruments and intrinsic voices in Burgess's writing are projected as direct but complicated expositions through either imposing a musical color over a sentence via extended descriptive imageries or through transmittance of a wide scale of instruments redrawn midst similes and metaphors with textual descriptions of their effective roles.

The hoodwinked protagonist "Tristram Foxe" in Burgess's *The Wanting Seed* (1962) who finds himself a Sergeant in the new British Army; is orchestrated as member of a choral mass right in the front line teaching conscripts. The mass of the army's melancholic state is depicted as a sentimental overture to the later approaching sounds of artillery and explosions, on a familiar (monotonic) but unknown (Evasive cadence)land through which they sing songs of camaraderie as they uneasily listen to sketchy reports of (contrapuntal) enemy Activities. Such mood of the soldiers below the decks of troopships is being extended to readers by one of them playing a vernacular instrument; the "most melancholy of instruments-a mouth-organ. They sang; we'll be coming home, coming home, coming home, someday soon, January of June. Evening, morning, or afternoon..." (240) In a parallel instance, that is in Benjamin Britten's opera "Billy Budd" the oppositional forces of an extensive tonal atmosphere are condensed within the tenor voice (the highest male voice within the modal register) of the all-male shanties below decks on the ship "Indomitable" according to which the attack of the French ship is chromatically impending. In comparison to *The Wanting Seed*'s tenor army that sings on a metaphorically unknown "accompaniment" of land, in Billy Budd's last act, captain 'Vere of Indomitable' representing the tenor voice of authorship is polyphonically attracted to the baritone (The male singing voice, between the bass and tenor) of Billy Budd off stage, when the orchestra suggests a tender instrumental dialogue between them as the captain informs Billy of the death sentence. In both examples, tenor as a decisive musical figure of speech and which is also applied to instruments, such as the tenor saxophone, is estranged dialogically to its counter baritone indicating the imminent storm of engagement with the enemy, whether it is vocally choral as with "The Wanting Seed's" "elevator music" or instrumentally dialogical as in "Billy Budd".

In *The Wanting Seed* moreover, is a dictive heteroglossia of Burgess's own instrument, the piano. In the latest part of the textual scale, the marching soldiers are required to shift their background noise —musically justified as a subsequent ornament-to a temporal hiatus;" Fall out'. They fell out; the duller men found out quickly what that long word meant; the road was cozy with the comfortable warm noise of hissing" (250) according to which the mechanism of the piano's left pedal which causes reduction of tonal sharpness and power is depicted as a figurative simile "from tre corde to una corde." (251)Accordingly, the previous diminuendo -a tempo mark directing that a passage is to be played gradually more softly-descending on the evasive cadence of the unknown land, has finally found an alternate on the piano's left pedal-with a permanent prophecy of an outside/external hiss; "where doesn't mean anything. It's just a bit of land, that's all."(251) They could hear motor noises in crescendo (opposite to diminuendo) on the road outside the camp. In addition, an instrumentalist or a musical competent is the most likely to benefit when listening to atypical or early instruments in the same novel ,that is, when "gulls" are mentioned to be "cackling like heckle-phones"(280) with which the redundant monotone of cackling is metaphorically instrumented to a baritone large oboe of a same alliteration.

In relation to Burgess's unconventional realization of his instrument the piano, which is put into his texts as means of autotelic musicality, there should be as well a reference to a violin-bow technique intrinsic in the accusation of the *Tremor of Intent* (1966) protagonist; Hillier to be a spy who "like a violinist confidently down-bowing in with the rest of the section, started to laugh. But nobody else laughed. Hillier was playing from the wrong score."(60) Incidentally so, the forceful implication of the protagonist's first arrangement of his entry has proven to be miscalculated and the hammering effect of the bow's martellato (accented effect, where flexible fingers and wrist are a must) comes in a singular unattended passage as perplexedly exposed as the helpless protagonist Hillier.

In addition to Burgess's contribution to the musicality of instrumental punctuated accents and choral voice, there should be a sequential reference to the musical terms and specific techniques he utilized in his writings, mainly novels, which cover a range of complex resonances and extended metaphors from eponymous classical scales (set of musical notes ordered by fundamental frequency or pitch) till revolutionary compositional methods. In his novel *The Worm and the Ring* (1961), Burgess applies an arrangement of the original concept of the musical scale, the octatonic-which contains normally 8 tones per octave-when the homosexual Mr.Turton is conceptualized as "Turton the exquisite, with his chromatic scale of giggles."(61) The chromatic scale is a tonal scale of twelve pitches; with each semitone/half tone above or below another, and in the aforesaid reference the indicated tonal intervals that normally categorize each scale are compared to the half human vocal register (giggle) underlying silence while trespassing smile. It chromatically would lead (reading) listeners virtually to the highest pitched soprano (the highest singing voice) of laughter. So far, as the mentioning of the word "worm" (an archaic word for dragon) is marginalized throughout the novel, though it represents the novel's only pub "The Dragon pub" –as there is also little mention in the book of either worms or rings- the book becomes but Burgess's own version of the Ring Cycle (a cycle of four epic operas by the German composer Richard Wagner (1813-83)) which is compared in the novel to a stolen ring. But, is Burgess's book is just a diatonic retelling of Richard Wagner's own cycle? Burgess justified his own position saying that "In a symphony many strands conjoined, in the same instant, to make a statement; ...The ease with which dialogue could be written seemed grossly unfair." (Biswell, The Real Life of Anthony Burgess, 92) and even more he turned against the conventional definition of stealing, stating that "It seemed cheating not to be able to give the reader chords and counterpoint. It was like pretending that there could be such a thing as a concerto for unaccompanied flute."(92) For him thus, music unlike writing could never be accused of plagiarism or theft, so far as it depends more or less on the final approach of the listeners' taste, not a counter-theory.

In concert with the chromatic scale and Burgess's musical relationship to revolutionary compositional methods is *The Complete Enderby* (1963) characters' counterpoint to the idea having been plagiarized;" Enderby prepared twelve obscene English words as a ground row." (Inside Mr.Enderby, 159) In the later quote there is an irrevocable reference to the expressionist Austrian composer and painter Arnold Schoenberg (1874-1951) and his development of the twelve-tone technique in the 1920s. It is a methodical form of serialism according to which the 12 notes of the chromatic scale sounded as one another in a musical piece without emphasis on any one note. It is a reordering of the 12 pitches where all of

5

them are given approximately equal importance and thus the music avoids being in a major or minor key. It is virtually comparable to the collective identity approach in literature apparent in novels like *The Light House* by Virginia Wolfe. Such compositional method is accomplishable through the use of tone-rows (also a serious that refers to a non-repetitive arrangement of pitches). Enderby's mentioning of a "twelve English words" as a "ground row" intricately imposes on words' intonation a process of semantic variation which is normally achievable by the twelve tones technique. There is a stress on the dialogical multifarious nature of "obscene" words that could be analogically attributed to the continuous variation of the indicated tones, right without repetition but with equal condensation of meaning. Moreover, as the chromatic scale does segment its tones systematically in an ascending or descending manner, "obscene" words could comparatively be epitomized to resemble ascending or descending modes of obscenity –right from a slightest non-verbal offence to its extreme polyphonic practice- towards the intended subject. In addition, crescendo or diminuendo as modes of tonal pressure along a tonal variable could imaginatively be replayed by readers to add or deduct depth from its pyrrhic musicality.

The term "petro-musicology" which appears in the third of the Enderby novels indicates one of Burgess' provisional inventions of a soon-to-be-refined branch of musicology. In his own words, Enderby the protagonist at New York University condemns the teaching of petro-musicology;" What had been a center of incorrupt learning was now a whorehouse of progressive intellectual abdication...this being so-called a democracy; courses in soul-cookery, whatever that was, and petromusicology , that being teenage garbage now treated as an art.." (*Burgess,The Clockwork Testament*, 413)However, when the newly invented term is symbolically compared to its Greek root "petra" and to "petrology" (The branch of science concerned with the origin, structure, and composition of rocks), it could be contemplated that The Rolling Stones band which inaugurated the British Invasion phenomena (when "rock" and pop music from the United Kingdom became overwhelmingly popular in the United States) lies behind it. A modernist classical composer like Anthony Burgess could then be introduced as an exemplified hater of rock music that could have been equally expelled by prominent antecedent composers of "Waltz of Snowflakes" in Tchaikovsky's Nutcracker or "After the Rain" by Erik Satie.

Another contribution of Anthony Burgess to extend the musical experience in his writings right in between lines semantically, symbolically and instrumentally, is the cinematic technique adept at imposing sound to sight when elaborating definitions of settings and describing pictorial entries. Burgess's novel *The Worm and the Ring* (1954)for example, introduces such audio-visual experience right from the beginning of affirming Burgess's own belief considering difficult words' representations and neologisms;" My notion of giving the reader his money's worth was to throw difficult words at him ...to give the impression of a musicalisation of prose." (*The Real Life of Anthony Burgess*, 99) In *The Worm and the Ring* novel there is a detonation of musical consonance (Sets of tones that are harmonious when sounded together)indicating the end of a school's exhausting day and which referred to loquaciously as a final practice of an orchestral ensemble: "..mad electric bells spelling release...treble laughter[in the cloak rooms]...guffaws running rang under the showers...[there were] flushing cisterns ,hissing taps..." (3)At a first reading it could be justifiable to musically taste meanings' sequence as an entire tonal disarrangement condensed through intentional repetitions of a Presto progression (A signature in sheet music indicating that the tempo is to be played very fast.) as in " mad"," running", "rang", "flushing". However, the structural release of such homophonous dynamics apparent in rhythmic motifs as in "showers","flushing","taps" counter-balance the first fermatas (To hold a tone beyond the written value) of discordance to a final legato (ligature)with temperament (relates to the tuning of an instrument.)

Among Anthony Burgess's works that deal with audio-visual approach quiet painfully in terms of its recitative musicality (a writing for vocals, closer to the manner of speech and is rhythmically free) is the fictional biography of William Shakespeare; *Nothing Like the Sun* (1964) where at some point Shakespeare strolls through London streets distractedly while composing a dedication to the Earl of Southampton. In his dilemma of revising and correcting his own words, Shakespeare's attention is frequently caught by the interfering sounds of Elizabethan England in a ritually musical connotation closer to glissando-that depends on sliding between two notes-and according to which his poetic transcription becomes too much lyrical in its capriccio to deliver cordially the intended passage. Shakespeare accordingly becomes a promoter of an assumable cadence when he says; "Piemen and flower-sellers cried...in dedicating my lines, no, my unpolished lines, to your lordship...From a barber-shop came the tuning of a lute and then the aching sweetness of treble song... "(97) The comparative tuning of the classical lute as a string instrument to the self of Shakespeare as a perfectly tuned classical writer indicates the state of improvisation that works as a transitional stage from the prolific cadenza of dedication (an improvised cadence by a soloist; elaborately played in an aria or concerto) to an experimental seriousness of a caprice (The bewildered Shakespeare).

Still in consequence to the auditory impetus as an empirical component in Burgess's musicality-right from simple weaving of arcane symbolism to aesthetically experimental dodecaphony (Twelve-tone technique), is the contrastive experience of Hillier's first experience of a Russian coastal city to Shakespeare's Elizabethan England. Instead of the interlude's musical theft of the canonical cadence from Shakespeare ,in so far as to capture his own script midst dedicational composition and imposing imperative improvisation, Hillier in "Tremor of Intent" is totally disarmed from his instrumental independence and robbed moreover structurally from his application of an eschatological espionage. Now encore (music played at the end of a recital in response to an enthusiastic reaction from audience) is proven to have encountered the protagonist's negative status as a spy by a scandal of espressivo fugue (a musical note written for three to six voices. Beginning with the exposition, each voice enters at different times) as in his own description of the city; "Someone has cleared his voice with vigor. A dog barked, miles away, and set other dogs barking...trolley-hissing and clanks of trams...treetops susurrated in the breeze...Perhaps a band played the state-directed circus-music of Aram Khachaturian..."(119) Six subjects of a textual fugue are hereby presented as a musical background to an episodic exposition, starting from a vocal tenor as the protagonist's own highest dexterity in his determination to write ,to imminent tones' entries of different coloratura (elaborate ornamentation of a vocal line) that no sooner had they conjoined his own inspiration than their condensed fermatas – tones held beyond the written value-started to disown their vocal artist and leaving him miserably discolored/ out of rhyme.

In line with significant references to instrumental dialogues and compositional from-early-to mid-20th century's selected terms and serial techniques, a derivational configuration of new musical devices should forwardly be emphasized as analogous to real musical instruments promoting a sensation of syntactic novelty and onomatopoeia. *In The Worm and the Ring* there is an indication of an eponymous but familiar tone proven to be achievable by a concurrent tapping on the table; "Howarth drank from his glass of cloudy Pernod and a thorn of ice hit a tooth like a tuning-fork."(175) If the sound of an ice's hit is a tonal familiarity in terms of color why there should be a reference to the tuning device of pitch? As a Walt Disney's cartoon character could at its climacteric incident be attributed in his tumbles to a rolling piano's portamento (a slide from one note to another) insofar as to visualize the musical significance to its comic extreme capacity, a jingling tooth could accordingly be aurally tuned to its visual attribution right after a committing of a tumbling – unintentional-forte (A symbol indicating to play loud) by a reluctant thorn. Though an interjection of an auditory pitch within a descriptive passage could be a textual impossibility-although attainable through meticulous considerations of words syntax which would turn in the end to be a conventional materialization of tonal exposition-the intentional compartment of the thorn with its hit has substituted the intended pitch for a similar "visual" interest, and a similar measure.

In an identical reference to musical devices as narrative figures, a hidden motif seems to weave an apparent reference to the "tuning-fork" right with its legislative counterpart-that is through an informal pun- according to which a series of semantic disembodiments attains its last musicality. In "Enderby Outside"- the second volume in the Enderby series – while Enderby decides to flee the city in fears of being charged with murder and in the process he had to work his way out onto the plane to Morocco by bribing, he "lick-counted the money out. A good slice of his savings...Savings. The word struck, like a thin tuning-fork,...a pertinent connotation." (236) The addition of the word 'thin' right to the tuning-fork could be 'chromatically' justified only when rendered to its functionality on an instrument in "thin", pure, separate mode. A thin tuning-fork produces a sound of "a same pitch" when played on an instrument or even sung, but it revealingly ends with an equally powerful resonance of a multi-layered implication which the first state of the fork has disowned. This process ends in a parallel connotation to the Enderby's "savings" whose own doubled significance would help him to escape a charge of murder. The pun here then carries a musical device as a derivative of functionality while the tuning-fork implies the possible application of its complete 'denouement'.

In *Inside Mr. Enderby* though, which is the first of Enderby novels, there is a stylistic excursion –a probable process of identifying a musical acquired taste as a first listener's perplexity before notation- from instrumental deciphering to metaphorical appreciation when Enderby appears as to have to experience a poor poem, conceived to be "read out, with a voice pitched high and on one tuning-fork note." (49) Reminiscently speaking, there is a catachresis to the way many poets overrate their poems' lack of subject with much orchestrated (fake) inexpressiveness that is ,in other words, to substitute rhythm for pitch or the main color with mordent ornaments (rapid alternation between an intended note, the note above or below, and the intended note again). The tuning-fork in this example has been proven to be a recurrent motif of a double significance right from its complete functionality of tuning-that is of obtaining its complete application on an instrument-through the thin tuning-fork technique with its "savings" mode according to which significance is systematically delivered from the fork, right to its external "pertinent connotation" and ends so far with its high-pitched inexpressiveness according to which the tuning-ford turns not to be itself tuned.

To resume the idea of textual instrumentation as a complete process that entangle a given script right from its symantec subjectivity to an experimental semiotic considerations, there should be an initial reference to one of Burgess's most domineering quotes in his novel *This Man and Music* (2001) as concerns his own classification of language and hereafter its own direct or indirect relationship to the methodical tonality (stabilities and attractions); "The easily filmable novel belongs to a category which I shall call Class 1 fiction."(147) In Class 1 fiction "language is a zero quantity"(156), transparent, unseductive, where thoughts offer vehicles of meanings and structures easily heard from a monotonous mouth of tone whose ultimate capabilities are but to offer a performative prescription to musical and unmusical readers equally, with no rhapsodic taste for the normal decipherer, nor an eloquent scale for a thankful player. The structure has no meaning outside the actions of the plot which sustain it, or which it sustains. Class 1 fiction for Anthony Burgess is thus unmusical and therefore excluded from his natural musical preferentiality although quiet its mentioning is much significant to stress on Burgess' own contrastive mode that exposes his own talent as a case of choice rather than a matter of instinct.

How language could operate itself then, performing a "formal trickery" (Gourevitch, *The Art of Fiction*, The Paris Review: Interviews 48) through which amateur and professional musicians become equalized as contributors to their own satisfaction on its own merits? Burgess's answer to one of his interviewers whose question stressed on "formal trickery" as whether its musical analogy is exhibited heavily by composers and if it is best understood by at least an amateur musician, went as follows" I think that music does teach practitioners in other arts useful formal devices, but the reader doesn't have to know their provenance.

Here's an example. A composer modulates from one key to another by the use of the "punning" chord, the augmented sixth (punning because it is also a dominant seventh)." (48) It could be discerned then in his former answer a first characteristic of class 2 fiction's language which is an "awe-inspiring virtuosity of language" whose "opacity" is "exploited" if not by musical reader's competency, be it by the "formal trickery" of a technical "pun". Reminiscently, it is obvious how different musical statements and meanings would lead to an extended 'cadence' have they entangled different contexts, that is for them to attribute for a musical universality of 'ambience'.

In his own words Burgess reverberated such musical extension when he referred to Joyce's *Ulysses* affirming to be" the work I have to measure myself hopelessly against each time I sit down to write fiction." (200)To co-stimulate both musical textual extension together then with 'formal trickery', Enderby for example is depicted as "hypnotized by the gash-gold-vermilion of the electric fire"(Inside Mr Enderby,40) which draws readers elegantly to the final section of Hopkin's poem "The Wind-hover" ;" Fall, gall themselves, and gash gold-vermillion." (40) In this form of extension-beyond tessitura- right from a script to a poem ,there is a formal trickery intrinsic within the word "fall" —that could only be terminologically justified in music as a pun- which refers to the technique "minor fall", when a chord's transition from the major fifth to the minor sixth creates a brooding tension and intensity in a song's verse, creating when ended again with a major lift a "gall", fiery protrusion equal to Enderby's odd poet or Hopkin's steady Christ. This formal trickery could be still —in Burgess's view- away from disoriented readers, however, in the same interview Burgess stressed that "fantasies enacted can follow a realistic exposition with neither explanation nor transitional device"(The Art of Fiction, Paris Review, Interviews, 49) which would lead common readers feeling more associated with clear-cut expositions such as " gash-gold vermillion" and to start questioning the intent relying behind its co-existent repetition. As it has been formerly said, Burgess advocated a qualified music on the merits of its intra-textual 'repetition', and thus what appears to mean only a color in "gold-vermillion", could be given a musical definition —by normal readers-by the fact that it is repeated. They would come to the definition of the "Musical Color" without being musicians which is; the repetition of characteristics of a tone that excurses it from others of a same pitch and volume. They could distinguish not only the characteristic of a musical color when it is repeated, but it could also be included that Endeby's "gold-vermillion" color is different from Hopkin's one, and surely by comparison readers would become "hypnotized."

If Burgess's language has in a way or another been proven to be a trap for literary conjugations, what else would often trespass readers' involvement in terms of musical delicacy away from analogical terms? Burgess, explicitly, stated to his interviewer that" As for the reader having to know about music—it doesn't really matter much...my instinct tells me to use vocabulary that is not much different from our own." (The Art of Fiction,50)

As concerns vocabulary in his language, we could perceive that Burgess's individual words attain their optimum by the context in which they progress, as the consonants' effect in "clumsy clacking...a tiny clank of centimes...handfuls of small tinkle"(276) do appear in "Enderby Outside". In these words, there is an obvious 'onomatopoeia' whose dedication to their verbal music converts simple vocabulary to simpler sense of percussions, derivational from alliteration in their plosives /K/ ,/T/.

In *The Wanting Seed* however, there is often a rhythm within characters' verbosity which adds extensions to their rhyming vocabulary in an episode-like fragmentations;"Tristram was caught in the crowd, borne irresistibly, apples to ripe, through the town, home of a swan, and nuts be grown, and a lexicographer, petticoats up...and trousers down"(180) Before the mentioning of the former quotation, Tristram in the text-being caught up in the crowd- had thrown an scordatura-al hint to systemize intuitive understanding as concerns the way the procession, which was following a brass band, sings, in so far that he said that it "plays a jaunty six-eight tones." "Six-eight tones" refers in the first place to the Dactylic Hexameter, which is a form of meter in poetry as a rhythmic scheme consisted of lines made from six ("hexa") feet. In the most uniform dactylic hexameter, each of these feet would be a dactyl (a long syllable followed by two or three short syllables). In this formal analogy, per-formative music could be excluded and be replaced by readers' understanding of poetry's metric form, without which vocabulary can innocently apply "trickery" upon those who may attribute such analogy to only musical scales. In due to application of a six-eight tones on Tristram's words, long syllables will hereby be marked by < and the short by >. Accordingly then, part of the aforesaid quotation could be read as such; "Tri>stam< was<, caugh>tin< the< crow<d, born>e ire<sis<tib<ly, a>ppl<est<o ri<pe..."

In an attempt to extract an example of Burgess's serious cynicism out of his diction's timbre, it could be significant to proffer one of his quotes about language that justify implicitly syntactical difficulties to be sometimes the author's musical rehabilitation of his novels' skeptic characters. In his words he happened to declare that" The ideal reader of my novels is a lapsed Catholic and failed musician, short-sighted, color-blind, auditorily biased..." (The Art of Fiction, 52) Comparatively, Enderby who has renounced poetry in "Enderby Outside" as an adolescent occupation, been divorced as well as having his works plagiarized, and named Hogg-in his process of self-rehabilitation- is exposed to complex features of a man he comes across in his psychiatrist's reception described as" a man with wild grey hair who spoke with a cultivated accent which made his demotic vocabulary seem affected...being rehabilitated as in the same modes as Hogg himself had been, if he really had been, it probably was." (207)In such example, musicians would" hear the discord" in between the binary "cultivated accent" and "the demotic vocabulary" but fail to associate it to a musical analogy as the "vocabulary seem affected" and thus informally "tricked". Non-musician readers, on the other hand would be trapped within Enderby-Hogg's mental uncertainty, and the vocabulary's twisted syntax would take them away from formal, precise musical discordance in an abyss of incoherence. In short, musicians are led from acknowledged discordance to trickery, while non-musicians from unacknowledged discordance to incoherence.

It could be surprising and unsurprising however for musicians and non-musicians to have Burgess's Sonata for Cello and Piano in G Minor been discovered after it was thought to be lost for more than 60 years, in April 2011, which has recently been confirmed to be technically mature, per-formatively melancholic, in a sharp contrast to musically humorous syntax in his own novels. It is as if reverberating Burgess's saying that" Language exists less to record the actual than to liberate the imagination." (Ballard, *The Best Short Stories of J. G. Ballard*, Introduction) It could be seriously perceived as blame to those who have overrated his comic prolificacy in his experimental writing and substituted his verbose history for an aspect of a polite death. In many ways, this Sonata which would expose some impacts of the Second World War on him, and which was originally written "For the Dead", "does have one thing in common with his novels – a great story." (Cain, Anthony Burgess: Melancholy music from a Humorous Novelist, 1)The dystopian satire which marks most of Anthony Burgess's novel is now resumed by a clock-worked retort. Fortunately!

Works Cited

.Burgess, Anthony. Enderby outside. London: Heinemann, 1968. Print

.Burgess, Anthony. Inside Mr. Enderby. London: Heinemann, 1975. Print

Burgess, Anthony. Joysprick: An Introduction to the Language of James Joyce. London: .Deutsch, 1973. Print

Burgess, Anthony. Nothing like the Sun, a Story of Shakespeare's Love-life. New York: W.W. .Norton, 1964. Print

.Burgess, Anthony. This Man and Music. London: Hutchinson, 1982. Print

.Burgess, Anthony. Tremor of Intent. New York: Norton, 1966. Print

.Burgess, Anthony. The Wanting Seed. New York: W.W. Norton &, 1963. Print

Burgess, Anthony. The Worm and the Ring. London: Heinemann, 1970. Print

Cain, Matthew. "Cain on Culture." Cain on Culture Anthony Burgess Melancholy Music from a Humorous Novelist Comments. Http://blogs.channel4.com, 10 Nov. 2012. Web. 10 Oct. ..2013

.Ellmann, Richard. Ulysses on the Liffey. New York: Oxford UP, 1972. Print

Gourevitch, Philip. The Paris Review: The Art of Fiction,Interviews. New York: Picador, 2006. .Print

.Joyce, James. Ulysses. New York: Random House, 1946. Print

.Woolf, Virginia. To the Light-house. London: Panther, 1983. Print